TABLE OF
CONTENTS

LET'S MAKE SOME MONEY!

Everyone loves payday—from the first quarter you earned for setting the table to the weekly allowance you squirrelled away to buy toys or iPhone apps. Then comes the day of that first official paycheck and all of the responsibility that comes with it.

ALL ABOUT THE GREEN

The Teens' Guide to Finding Work and Making Money

by KARA McGUIRE

COMPASS POINT BOOKS
a capstone imprint

Compass Point Books are published by Capstone,
1710 Roe Crest Drive, North Mankato, Minnesota 56003
www.capstonepub.com

Editorial Credits
Angie Kaelberer and Catherine Neitge, editors; Ted Williams, designer;
Eric Gohl, media researcher; Laura Manthe, production specialist

Image Credits
Alamy: Jeff Greenberg 5 of 6, 47; Courtesy of Mik Mart Ice Cream: 34; Faye
Rusk/Junior Achievement of Southeast Texas: 36; Getty Images: Ethan
Miller, 39 (bottom), FilmMagic/Taylor Hill, 38 (top); Newscom: Dan Harr/
AdMedia, 9, Getty Images/AFP/Joe Klamar, 38 (bottom); Public Domain:
51; Shutterstock: Annette Shaff, 39 (top), baranq, 24–25, bikeriderlondon, 4–5,
Brian A Jackson, 18–19, Carla Donofrio, 14–15, Edyta Pawlowska, 29, Golden
Pixels LLC, 41, Goodluz, 17, hxdbzxy, 10, iQoncept, 22, isak55, 44–45, Kheng
Guan Toh, 42–43, kurhan, 58–59, michaeljung, 27, NicoElNino, 52, ollyy,
cover, 54–55, Peshkova, 30–31, photobank.ch, 12 (background), PTstock, 50
(background), Quka, 56, Sergey Nivens, 1, wavebreakmedia, 32–33

Design Elements: Shutterstock

Library of Congress Cataloging-in-Publication Data
McGuire, Kara.
  All about the green: the teens' guide to finding work and making money /
by Kara McGuire.
    pages cm.—(Compass point books. Financial literacy)
    Includes bibliographical references and index.
    ISBN 978-0-7565-4372-3 (library binding)
    ISBN 978-0-7565-4929-9 (paperback)
    ISBN 978-0-7565-4937-4 (eBook PDF)
  1. Vocational guidance—Juvenile literature. 2. Wages—Juvenile literature.
  3. Teenagers—Finance, Personal—Juvenile literature. I. Title.
  HF5381.2.M42 2015
  650.140835—dc23   2014003739

Printed in the United States   5628

That includes spending wisely and saving for the future. It means making smart decisions but still having fun. Learn all about the ins and outs of making money—from paychecks to paying taxes, finding jobs, and starting businesses. And best of all, learn how to earn money without lifting a finger.

CHAPTER ONE

JOBS AND
CAREER PLANNING

It's common for teens to juggle schoolwork and paid work, whether it's the occasional babysitting job or waiting tables 20 hours a week at a restaurant. Teens need money for hanging out, for hobbies, or for gas for the car. Then there is the cost of big things, such as saving for a car, helping with college tuition, or taking an overseas trip with the school orchestra. It's understandable why sometimes earning money seems more important than keeping up grades or working on college applications.

EDUCATION AND EARNINGS

Your number one job as a teen is to get good grades, gain experiences from school and community activities, and prepare for higher education. Your education affects job opportunities and how much you will be able to earn. The lifetime median earnings of a worker with just a high school diploma is $1.3 million. It may sound like a ton of money today, but it averages to $15 per hour—that's not much once you consider daily expenses and how long you could live. Americans with a bachelor's degree can plan on median lifetime earnings of $2.3 million. Those who stay in school for a doctoral or professional degree, such as medicine or law, earn a median of $3.6 million.

Although there are certainly exceptions to this rule, having a bachelor's degree increases your chances of earning more money and opens more doors to interesting, fulfilling careers. As the chart indicates, nearly 80 percent of people who earn $200,000 a year or more have a bachelor's degree or higher. Less than 10 percent of people at that income level have only a high school education.

If a four-year college is not in your plans, some people, such as electricians, construction managers, and sales managers, have average lifetime earnings that come close to the earnings of workers with bachelor's degrees.

WELL-EDUCATED AMERICANS HAVE HIGH INCOMES

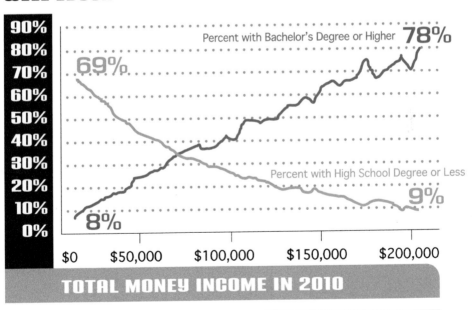

Percent with Bachelor's Degree or Higher 78%

69%

Percent with High School Degree or Less 9%

8%

$0 $50,000 $100,000 $150,000 $200,000

TOTAL MONEY INCOME IN 2010

Source: Census and http://taxfoundation.org/article/who-are-americas-millionaires#_ftn5

WHAT IS A COLLEGE MAJOR WORTH?

Here's something to think about when you go off to college. The average starting salary for college grads in 2014 was $45,473.

HERE'S THE AVERAGE BY MAJOR:

>**BUSINESS: $53,901**

>**COMMUNICATIONS: $43,924**

>**COMPUTER SCIENCE: $61,741**

>**EDUCATION: $40,863**

>**ENGINEERING: $62,719**

>**HEALTH SCIENCES: $51,541**

>**HUMANITIES AND SOCIAL SCIENCES: $38,365**

>**MATH AND SCIENCES: $43,414**

Source: National Association of Colleges and Employers Salary Survey, April 2014
https://www.naceweb.org/uploadedFiles/Content/static-assets/downloads/executive-summary/2014-april-salary-survey-executive-summary.pdf

HOW MUCH $$$ DOES IT TAKE TO BE HAPPY?

Hank Williams Jr.

"Mo money, mo problems."
—BIGGIE SMALLS

"Well now, money can't buy you happiness, but neither can poor ole me."—HANK WILLIAMS JR.

Hank and Biggie were wrong. More money does not automatically equal more problems. And while you can't buy happiness with cold, hard cash, researchers have found that when people expand their income, they report more life satisfaction, no matter how much money they start with.

WHEN WILL YOU BE A MILLIONAIRE?

That's right—not if, but when. You can earn more than $1 million in your lifetime by following these tips.

1. Stay in school. Keep learning, whether it's college or a training program for a good job.

2. Know where your money goes. Track your spending and have a plan for your money. If you don't, you'll be surprised at how quickly it disappears.

3. Start saving. Because of the magic of compound interest, the earlier you start to save, the more your money will grow. Even putting aside a few dollars each paycheck is worthwhile.

4. Spend smart. If you spend nearly as much or more than you make, you'll have a hard time reaching seven-figure savings. Research before you buy and consider needs, wants, and long-term goals before shopping.

5. Take calculated risks. Dream big. Try new things. Don't be afraid to fail. But make sure the risks you're taking make sense and fit with your overall life plan.

LLIONAIRE
LCULATOR
There's an easy online calculator for
uring how long it will take to earn $1 million,
pending on the savings plan and amount
ved per year. Check it out at themint.org.

Source: http://www.themint.org/kids/when-will-you-be-a-millionaire.html

While being a student is your primary job, paid work comes with benefits beyond a paycheck. A job can teach you responsibility, time management, teamwork, keeping commitments, and managing money. These are lessons you'll use throughout life. They also come in handy for writing college application essays and deciding on a future career.

Balancing work and school is a juggling act that requires support from your family and an organizational plan. Some ideas to keep you balanced include:

- *Keep a calendar of school and work commitments and consult the calendar before making plans.*

- *Stick to a weekly schedule, if possible, working the same number of hours and days.*

- *Start slowly. This will prevent overcommitting to work hours you can't handle.*

- *Ask your boss if you can use down time at the job to do schoolwork. But don't count on down time. When you're at work, the job comes first.*

- *If work is interfering with your success at school, you'll have to cut back on work.*

Jobs—what's HOT

The following jobs are the 10 fastest-growing occupations between now and 2022, according to the U.S. Bureau of Labor Statistics.

Source: http://www.bls.gov/ooh/fastest-growing.htm

OCCUPATION	GROWTH RATE	2012 MEDIAN PAY
Industrial-organizational psychologists	53 percent	$83,580
Personal care aides	49 percent	$19,910
Home health aides	48 percent	$20,820
Insulation workers, mechanical	47 percent	$39,170
Interpreters & translators	46 percent	$45,430
Diagnostic medical sonographers	46 percent	$65,860
Construction helpers*	43 percent	$28,220
Occupational therapy assistants	43 percent	$53,240
Genetic counselors	41 percent	$56,800
Physical therapist assistants	41 percent	$52,160

* Brickmasons, blockmasons, stonemasons, and tile and marble setters

Flatbed Expe
48 States

GENERAL
FULL TIME 9
CLERK POSITI

GENERAL

OFFICE HELP
Seeking energetic
& positive people.
Excellent pay!
motions available.

OOR WORK

FINDING A JOB

Having fun money is tops on teens' lists of reasons for getting a part-time job. Saving for college is important too.

But finding a part-time job can be challenging. The teen unemployment rate has stayed above 20 percent since the Great Recession of 2007–2009. You can look for a job through help-wanted ads in the newspaper, online at sites such as indeed.com or monster.com, or by searching for notices on bulletin boards or signs in storefronts.

If you don't find a job scooping ice cream or selling clothes at the mall, it's OK to ask around. Networking is an important skill and a common way for adults to find new opportunities. Ask your friends, people you know through school or extracurricular activities, your neighbors, and your family for ideas. The more people who know you're job-hunting and the kinds of opportunities that interest you, the more likely you'll find the perfect job.

If you can't find a paid position, consider an unpaid internship in a field you are interested in or volunteering for a cause you care about. Either experience will look great on a résumé and may give you a better idea of what college major or career field would be the perfect fit for you. If money is a must, try to earn some by starting your own business babysitting, mowing lawns, or using a specialized skill such as website development or playing an instrument.

Don't forget to highlight your work or volunteer experiences in your college applications and essays. Holding down commitments outside of school while excelling in your studies shows a strong work ethic and the ability to succeed under pressure. They are qualities college admissions officers like to see.

WORKING FOR EXPERIENCE

Sometimes when you're young and exploring careers, you won't be paid for your work. Internships can offer excellent experience and help narrow down the type of career you will find fulfilling and enjoyable. Same with job shadowing, where you find someone whose job sounds interesting and ask to spend some time understanding what he or she does. That may mean heading to the office for the day, tagging along on sales visits, or spending the day in a classroom or doctor's office watching what the employee does. You might help with some tasks, but often job shadowing is what it sounds like—you are that person's "shadow" for the day. In many cases you won't get paid for doing this. Yet the experience, knowledge, and connections are worth a great deal.

For some positions, such as a store sales clerk or a restaurant server, you'll fill out an application form for the hiring manager. If the manager thinks you might be a good fit for the job, the application will be used as a starting point for an interview.

For other jobs you will need a résumé. It is a one-page document designed to help you sell your background, skills, education, and qualifications for a job. You need a rock-star résumé to stand out from the crowd. After all, you want the hiring manager's first impression to be "wow," not "meh."

- *Your name and contact information*

- *Summary statement about why you want the job*

- *Work, internships, and volunteer experience*

- *Education, additional skills, and interests*

- *Honors and awards you've received*

While you'll have a standard résumé, you'll want to tweak it each time you apply for a new job so that it relates to that particular position. You'll also want to make sure your résumé is well written. No typos, poor grammar, or run-on sentences. Everything on a résumé must be accurate—no exaggerating or embellishing experience. Find a teacher, parent, or other adult to read your résumé and make suggestions before e-mailing or sending it to a potential employer. Collegeboard.com has good tips on writing a résumé. Job search site monster.com has sample résumés from many industries. If you are stuck, careerkids.com also has a questionnaire that will spit out a basic résumé for you.

You may also need to submit a cover letter, which summarizes why you want the job and what makes you a good candidate. Employers might also ask for references—people who can vouch for your character and experience. References are typically teachers, former co-workers, and adults who know you from volunteer or extracurricular settings.

Jane S. Doe
1234 Elm Street
Anytown, NY 12345
Phone: (123) 555-1234
E-mail:jsdoe@email.com

OBJECTIVE
To obtain a part-time position where I can use my computer and customer service skills.

EDUCATION
Anytown High School, Anytown, NY
Entering 11th grade, fall semester.
GPA 3.5
Classes taken include Spanish I and II, Accounting 1 and II, Computer Science, Web Design, and Introduction to Marketing.

EMPLOYMENT
June 2013–May 2014
Sales/Customer Service—KwikeeCopy, 555 1st Street, Anytown, NY
Processed jobs, maintained equipment, ordered supplies, answered phones, and provided customer service.

OTHER WORK EXPERIENCE
2010–Present
Babysitting
Provide part-time child care for groups of one to four children.

VOLUNTEER EXPERIENCE
September 2013–Volunteered at Anytown Boys' and Girls' Club carnival.

March 2014–Organized charity car wash for Anytown Animal Shelter, which raised $500.

SPECIALIZED SKILLS
- Proficient with Microsoft Office software, including web design.
- Proficient with all types of social media.
- Fluent in Spanish.
- Work well and communicate effectively with a variety of people, including supervisors, co-workers, and customers.

HONORS AND AWARDS
- Elected sophomore class representative, Anytown High School.
- Named to honor roll each semester of freshman and sophomore years.
- Elected treasurer of Anytown High School Spanish Club.

EXTRACURRICULAR ACTIVITIES
Enjoy tennis, knitting, dog training, reading, and computer games.

REFERENCES
Available on request.

One of the hardest parts of landing a job is over—you have an interview. But what do you say at that interview? How should you act? Remember that you only get one chance to make a first impression—and you want to show the interviewer your best possible self.

Get smart: Since you've landed an interview, chances are you've done your research and know a lot about the company and job you hope to do. If not, this is your next step. Most companies have Internet and social media sites. You can also check the website of your local newspaper for articles about the company. Do not go to the interview unprepared or misinformed.

Be on time: Being punctual is as important as getting smart, if not more so.

Put on your listening ears: Pay careful attention to the questions you are asked. Ask for clarification if necessary.

Make eye contact: It's as important as ever, even in the age of texting and remote workplaces.

Play it safe: Interviews are generally not the place to discuss politics or religion, or to flaunt your expert knowledge of urban slang.

Follow-up: You may think that once you say your good-byes, all you have to do is wait. But if you want to increase your odds of landing the job, you have one more chance to make a good impression. Send a thank-you letter as soon as you can, preferably the same day. Express your thanks for being interviewed. Take the opportunity to briefly remind the interviewer of your skills, highlight a good point you made in the interview (or forgot to make), and add a final thank-you.

While e-mail is common these days, taking the extra step of also mailing a note on nice stationery or a note card will make a longer-lasting impression. Address the note to the person who interviewed you. And take time to send a note, even if you know right away that you didn't get the position. There's always next time.

WHAT (NOT) TO WEAR: TEEN JOB INTERVIEW EDITION

Dress for success. That's a statement you've probably heard before. But what does it mean? Appropriate attire for the workplace will vary depending on the job. Some jobs have uniforms, making it easy to figure out what to wear. Without a uniform, knowing what to wear to work can be tricky. Almost every workplace has a dress code. When you go in for your interview, you will be able to see how employees are dressed.

But wait—how do you know what to wear to a job interview? Or more important, what NOT to wear?

Again, it will vary. If you're interviewing at an investment firm, chances are women wear skirts, dresses, or suits, and men might wear suits and ties. If you are interviewing at an advertising agency, outfits probably vary based on personal style, and many styles are acceptable. When in doubt, dress up, not down. Here are some other suggestions, especially if you're applying for an office job:

Just ask: Talk to the person setting up the interview about the workplace atmosphere and how people typically dress.

Don't wear jeans: In most cases wearing jeans to an interview is a no-no, even if jeans are acceptable in the workplace. Keep the sneakers at home too, even your best pair.

Don't wear jeans, unless ... : You are applying to work retail at a store that sells exclusively jeans. It's OK to tweak your style based on the merchandise and atmosphere of the store you're hoping will hire you. But don't go overboard.

Be conservative: No bra straps showing, no see-through clothing, nothing too tight, nothing too short.

Have fun: Being conservative doesn't mean boring. You can wear color, jewelry (but not too much bling), or patterns that let your personal style shine through.

No hats: Sorry, kids.

Accessorize: Always bring your résumé and any samples of your work.

Not seen, not heard: Keep the smartphones and tablets out of sight.

CHAPTER TWO

BEING YOUR OWN BOSS

. . . .

"You're not the boss of me!"

Almost every kid has uttered that sentence at one point. The idea of being free to do what you want and make your own decisions has appeal no matter how old you are. It's one reason why 11.5 million Americans have chosen to be entrepreneurs instead of working for someone else.

But running a small business is hard work. It takes a good idea, a business plan, start-up money, and more. So where to begin?

WOULDN'T IT BE COOL IF ...

The first step is coming up with an idea. Ideas come from all over the place—a frustration you've experienced, an opportunity you've uncovered, or a dream that awakens you in the middle of the night with an "aha" moment. But before you go too far with your idea, ask yourself the following questions:

- *How do I like to spend my time?*

- *How much time do I have?*

- *What are my strongest skills?*

- *What do others say I am good at?*

- *Can any of this translate into a moneymaking opportunity?*

Once you've come up with an idea, survey the landscape. Identify the need you're fulfilling. Check to see if there are other local businesses already doing what you're planning to do. If there is competition, how will you drum up business? How will your business be different or better?

Still convinced you have a good idea? Running your business will take a lot of time, dedication, and sacrifice. Be honest with yourself and ask the following questions:

- *Would you rather work on your business than play sports, act in the school play, or watch TV?*

- *Would you rather spend your money on your business instead of on clothes or other wants and desires?*

- *Do you realistically have the time it will take without jeopardizing your studies? School, after all, is your primary job. Will family and friends help you out?*

If you are still jazzed about the idea of running a business, work your way through the handy pre-business checklist on the next page. It's from the U.S. Small Business Administration (SBA).

- *What services or products will I sell? Where will I be located?*

- *What skills and experience do I bring to the business?*

- *What will I name my business?*

- *What equipment or supplies will I need?*

- *What insurance coverage will be needed?*

- *How much money, if any, will it cost to start my business? Will I need financing?*

- *What are my resources?*

- *How will I compensate myself?*

Once you've walked yourself through the questions and checklist on the previous pages, it's time to get it all down in a formal document called a business plan. The purpose of a business plan is to define your business, as well as your strategy for establishing the business, keeping it going, and reaching the goals you outlined. It's the game plan for your business vision.

The business plan will draw from all of the research you've already completed. The SBA has another handy checklist that shows what should be included in the business plan. Find it at the SBA website, http://archive.sba.gov/teens/.

Here's a peek at a few of the items on the list:

- Give a detailed description of the business and its goals.

- Discuss the advantages you and your business have over your competitors.

- Identify the customer demand for your product or service.

- Identify your market, its size, and its locations.

- Explain how your product or service will be advertised and marketed.

- Explain the pricing strategy.

- Decide the amount and source of initial capital (money) you'll need.

- Develop a monthly operating budget for the first year.

- Determine your breakeven point where your income will at least cover your expenses. Anything above that is profit.

- Explain how the business will be managed on a day-to-day basis.

- Account for the equipment necessary to produce your products or services.

IDEA, PLAN, FINANCE

Once you've come up with a business idea and written your plan, your next step is to put that plan into action. Figuring out the financing—how you're going to pay for the business—is usually a key piece of the plan. If your business is going to require outside capital, there are several ways to raise it:

- *Use personal savings and earnings. Many entrepreneurs don't pay themselves a salary for many months, if not years. They put their earnings back into the business instead.*

- *Ask for start-up funds from family or friends.*

- *Ask your peers using a crowdfunding site such as Kickstarter.com or a peer-to-peer lending site such as lendingclub.com.*

- *Apply for a bank loan.*

ICE CREAM DREAMS

Mik Bushinski's cool life revolves around ice time and ice cream.

Bushinski needed a summer job that would allow him to attend hockey practice and work out twice a day. When he couldn't find one, he started a business selling ice cream treats in his Woodbury, Minnesota, subdivision. That was five years ago. Now he's 20 and has expanded his business from a single ice cream minivan to multiple vehicles and an ice cream vending machine business. Here's his story:

Mik Bushinski

He looked for an unmet need: "We had lived in Woodbury for close to 20 years and hadn't seen ice cream trucks very often and knew the community was growing and had a lot of families with children, so it seemed like a good fit."

He found start-up capital: "I needed about $5,000 to get the business started. My uncle gave me a no-interest loan."

He had a goal: "My ultimate motivation was to be able to keep playing hockey at Shattuck-St. Mary's for my high school career, and I needed to be able to help with the cost of that."

He got a little help from his family: "In the second year I added a second truck, which my parents and brother helped run. Then last year my little sister got a truck and is now running that one. We got a professional logo last year and had it put on all of the trucks, and we professionalized our website. We ventured into the ice cream vending business (my little sister handles most of that), and we hire a few people to help out in the summer."

MIK'S ADVICE FOR BUDDING ENTREPRENEURS:

1. Find a product that you believe in and would buy yourself.
2. Be ready to put a lot of time into your own business.
3. Make sure you have a financial plan.

Isaiah Rusk of Houston, Texas, started his own retail business at age 15, after his friends kept asking for style advice.

The business plan:

"I can go to the thrift store, pick up things that are cool and post them on a website, and if they like it, they could buy it."

His start-up capital:

"I saved up. It took me several months to get what I needed."

Isaiah Rusk

His marketing plan:

"I got the word out through Twitter and Instagram and Tumblr. Most of my customers aren't even from my area."

How he juggles a business and school:

He shops on Friday after school or Saturday, restocks the store on Sunday, and sends out orders "after I do my homework."

Where he went for business advice:

The Junior Achievement organization and his mom, who is also an entrepreneur.

ISAIAH'S ADVICE TO ENTREPRENEURS:

1. "When you get some money, you can't just blow it all. Most of the time you've got to put it to the side. Certain things will come up and you have to pay."
2. "Be patient."
3. "Don't involve your friends."

Plan for the future: He said he hopes to expand his website "to maybe like a small store, not necessarily a chain store, but just a small store. But what I mainly focus on is my acting. You always have to have some sort of backup plan when you're trying to be an actor."

What does it take to be an ENTREPRENEUR?

Entrepreneurs need ... ZOG. Entrepreneurs need zest, optimism, and grit, according to Camp BizSmart blogger Peggy Gibbs.

"Zest is defined as living life with a sense of excitement, anticipation, and energy. ... Zest is essentially the courage, and self motivation to complete challenging situations and tasks. Optimism is a positive, 'Can Do Attitude,' about life, school and work. ... Train yourself to see solutions, not just problems. Grit is sticking with things over the very long term until you master them."

THEY SAID IT

"I've always believed that one woman's success can only help another woman's success."
—Gloria Vanderbilt, fashion designer and artist

"One of the huge mistakes people make is that they try to force an interest on themselves. You don't choose your passions; your passions choose you."
—Jeff Bezos, technology entrepreneur

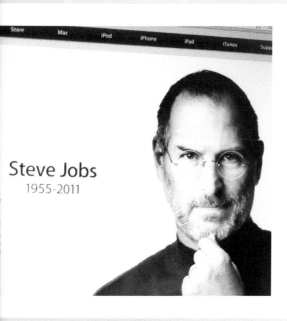

Steve Jobs
1955-2011

"Your time is limited, so don't waste it living someone else's life. Don't be trapped by dogma — which is living with the results of other people's thinking. Don't let the noise of other's opinions drown out your own inner voice. And most important, have the courage to follow your heart and intuition. They somehow already know what you truly want to become. Everything else is secondary."

—Steve Jobs, co-founder of Apple Computers

"I feel that luck is preparation meeting opportunity."
—Oprah Winfrey, billionaire media giant

CHAPTER THREE

WAGES
AND TAXES

Earning money is not just about an hourly wage, where you receive a certain amount of money for each hour on the job. There are various types of compensation. For example, you could earn a salary, which is a fixed amount of money you earn no matter how many hours you work per week. A salary is paid at regular periods, usually every other week or twice each month.

You may also work on commission, which means you are paid for completing certain tasks or reaching a goal. Commission is often tied to a sales goal.

Service workers often receive tips, which is money earned on top of a base wage because of a job well done or because of social convention. The consumer—the person being served—pays the tip. In some occupations, such as restaurant server and taxi driver, tips tend to be given regardless of the quality of the work. But remember that tips aren't mandatory and can fluctuate based on whether the consumer thinks you did a lousy job or a lovely one.

Is there a certain amount an employer must pay you? It depends. The United States has a minimum wage for most workers. That amount is currently $7.25 an hour. Congress must pass legislation to change it, although states can require businesses to pay a higher minimum wage. For example, workers making minimum wage in the state of Washington earn $9.32 per hour.

etter
wer

families women

trong

effective

changed

pay

mimum

jurisdictions

bor

e

Not all workers are paid minimum wage. Employers can pay workers who are younger than 20 a minimum wage of $4.25 per hour during their first 90 days on the job. Teens who babysit or are full-time students don't have to be paid minimum wage. If you receive tips on the job, you might not be paid minimum wage, depending on the amount of tips received. The U.S. Department of Labor website at http://www.dol.gov has all of the details.

EARNING MONEY IN YOUR SLEEP

Who wants to earn some money without lifting a finger? Who wouldn't raise their hand? The good news is that there are ways to watch your money grow over time without having to do much.

How? One of the best ways to earn money is by saving money in an account that earns interest.

Interest is money paid to someone who has agreed to let another party put their money to use for whatever purpose. When you open a savings account at a bank or credit union, you will be paid a small amount of interest for giving them your money and allowing them to use it for lending or other purposes. The interest paid is calculated as a percentage based on how much money you've deposited.

Where can you earn interest? In savings accounts, for sure. But there are also interest-earning options in college savings plans called 529 plans and tax-free Individual Retirement Accounts (IRAs), which are designed to save for retirement.

GETTING BY WITH A LITTLE HELP FROM FRIENDS (AND STRANGERS)

Banks aren't the only places you can earn interest. You can act as the bank yourself, lending money to your family members, friends, or even complete strangers through peer-to-peer lending. Peer-to-peer lending is just what it sounds like. It's been happening for centuries, but the Internet makes it possible to bring together strangers living in various parts of the world to help each other reach their financial goals. This marketplace has grown a lot in recent years, as banks made it tougher for consumers to borrow money and have cut interest rates paid on savings accounts. The conditions forced consumers looking for loans and consumers looking to earn interest to seek alternatives outside of banks. Peer-to-peer lending was born.

Websites such as prosper.com and lendingclub.com act as marketplaces for people looking for money and people looking to earn interest by lending money. Lenders who have money to loan browse the website. They read descriptions of borrowers—people who need a loan. Lenders learn who the borrowers are, where they live, why they're asking for cash, and how likely it is that they will be able to pay back the loan. Lenders will receive a certain amount of interest in return for lending their money to borrowers.

Money isn't the only thing that you can lend in return for cash. Think about how many items you can rent in this society—apartment cars, lawn equipment, bikes, prom dresses, movies, and TV shows. If you own property people would pay to use, that's another way to earn money without doing a job or waiting for interest to build.

That first paycheck is a thrill. But wait—why does it look so small? Taxes. Social Security. Medicare. The cost of benefits. It doesn't take long to realize that your hourly wage and your take-home pay are not the same thing. The actual amount in your paycheck that you get to spend? That's your net pay. It's what you have left after your employer withholds all of the mandatory stuff such as federal and state income taxes, and the voluntary deductions such as retirement savings and some types of insurance premiums. Your pay before all of the deductions is called your gross pay—as in, bigger than it was before all of those deductions kicked in, or isn't it gross that my paycheck is so much smaller?

In all seriousness, taxes benefit society by raising money to fix roads, keep parks beautiful, and protect citizens during wars and at home. Taxes are mandatory, and you must pay taxes on the income that you earn. If you're an employee of a company, the company will take a percentage of your salary each month to pay for state and federal taxes and programs such as Social Security and Medicare. Think of Social Security as a government-sponsored plan that gives retirees and select others a small monthly paycheck. Medicare is the government-sponsored health care plan for those 65 years old or older. If you see the term FICA (Federal Insurance Contributions Act) on your paycheck, it's referring to these programs.

Your paycheck may also have deductions that aren't required by the government. The voluntary deductions include health, disability, and life insurance; benefits that reduce the cost of child care or work-related parking expenses; and company retirement plans.

WHAT GETS TAKEN OUT OF YOUR PAYCHECK?

FEDERAL INCOME TAX

- The amount withheld is based on taxable income, pay frequency, marital status, and the number of allowances claimed.

SOCIAL SECURITY

- Flat percentage deducted based on taxable income

- May appear on your paycheck as FICA

MEDICARE TAX

- Flat percentage deducted based on taxable income

- May appear on your paycheck as FICA

OTHER DEDUCTIONS

- Insurance policies that vary based on employer or state policy.

STATE INCOME TAX

- Based on your W-4 and/or state income tax form *

- Based on taxable income, marital status, and allowances

There are five common payroll deductions made from an employee's earnings:

X COMPANY
Anytown, CA

Earnings Statement

Social Security Number: 999-99-9999
Taxable Marital Status: Single

Jane S. Doe
1234 Elm Street
Anytown, CA 12345

EARNINGS	Rate	Hours	This Period
Regular	$10.00	40.00	$400.00
Overtime	$15.00	1.00	$15.00
Gross Pay			$415.00

DEDUCTIONS	Statutory	
	Federal Income Tax	$42.00
	Social Security	$17.43
	Medicare Tax	$6.02
	Other Deductions	$15.00
	State Income Tax	$17.00
Net Pay		$317.55

* Not all states have state income tax.

Source: http://nerdgraphics.com/wp-content/uploads/2012/02/payroll_and_tax_deductions.png

If you've used allowance or birthday money to buy toys, clothes, or video games, or even eaten at a restaurant, you've likely paid sales tax. Sales tax is a set rate, no matter who you are or how much money you make. Depending on the state where you live, some items, such as groceries or clothes, might not be subject to sales tax. But most things you buy in a store are taxed.

Income tax is different. The amount of money withheld from your paycheck for taxes depends on how much you earn. It generally increases as you earn more. When you start your job, your employer will have you fill out a W-4 form, which tells your employer how much money to withhold from your paycheck and send to the IRS. Your parents or guardians or your employer can help you fill out that short form.

Teens don't always earn enough to have to file an annual income tax return. But it's worth considering, because a refund may be waiting from the government.

22222	Void ☐	a Employee's social security number		For Official Use Only ▶ OMB No. 1545-0008			
b Employer identification number (EIN)				1 Wages, tips, other compensation		2 Federal income tax withheld	
c Employer's name, address, and ZIP code				3 Social security wages		4 Social security tax withheld	
				5 Medicare wages and tips		6 Medicare tax withheld	
				7 Social security tips		8 Allocated tips	
d Control number				9		10 Dependent care benefits	
e Employee's first name and initial		Last name	Suff.	11 Nonqualified plans		12a See instructions for box 12	
				13 Statutory employee ☐ Retirement plan ☐ Third-party sick pay ☐		12b	
				14 Other		12c	
						12d	
f Employee's address and ZIP code							
15 State Employer's state ID number		16 State wages, tips, etc.	17 State income tax	18 Local wages, tips, etc.	19 Local income tax		20 Locality name

W-2 Wage and Tax Statement **2014**
Form
Copy A For Social Security Administration — Send this entire page with
Form W-3 to the Social Security Administration; photocopies are **not** acceptable.
Do Not Cut, Fold, or Staple Forms on This Page

Department of the Treasury—Internal Revenue Service
For Privacy Act and Paperwork Reduction
Act Notice, see the separate instructions.
Cat. No. 10134D

Source: http://www.irs.gov/pub/irs-pdf/fw2.pdf

The income tax form is called a 1040. Young people can typically use the simpler 1040EZ form to file. To help you prepare that form, your employer will send you a W-2 Wage and Tax statement at the beginning of each year. The W-2 includes the wages and tips you earned during the previous year, as well as the taxes withheld.

Want to earn more money? Who doesn't? As you get older and expenses rise, you'll need to steadily increase your salary to maintain your investment goals and standard of living. Sometimes you'll be offered a raise or promotion for working hard and gaining more experience. Other times you'll have to make a case for why you should earn more money.

Negotiating a salary or raise can be nerve-wracking, especially the first time. If you're still receiving an allowance from your parents or guardians, you can test your negotiating skills by asking for an increase in the amount you receive.

When you're ready to ask for more money at work or at home, follow these tips:

- **Treat your employer with respect. That goes for Mom and Dad too.**

- *Come to the table with a number in mind. Do your research. If negotiating an allowance, ask your friends how much allowance they are paid and for what sorts of tasks. If you're employed, find out what other workers in similar jobs are making. Check websites such as salary.com, indeed.com, or glassdoor.com for general information. But don't ask your co-workers what they are making. Most employers consider this information confidential. Also, don't forget that cost of living is different depending on where you live. That means employers may pay more or less based on location. Check out a cost of living calculator, available on most salary websites.*

- *Your magic number? Don't share it right away, especially if you're in the midst of negotiating an initial salary. And don't tell potential employers exactly how much you've made in past jobs. You might feel as if you have to if asked, but revealing that number could lower your salary offer at the new job. Of course, if you're negotiating at an existing job or for your allowance, this rule doesn't apply.*

- *Consider how your responsibilities have changed or your quality of work has improved. Would you be willing to take on more work for the raise you're proposing?*

- *If you're negotiating your allowance and don't earn money based on specific chores, make the case for more cash by analyzing your expenses and explaining what has changed in your financial life that requires more allowance.*

- *Dissatisfied with the results of your negotiation? Tell your employer or parent or guardian that the number is lower than your expectations and ask how he or she settled on that figure. Or request a plan to improve your performance or add skills so you have a greater chance of receiving a raise the next time you ask.*

IT PAYS TO NEGOTIATE

People who don't negotiate their first salary could lose more than $500,000 in earnings from the time they start their career until they reach age 60, according to statistics compiled by Linda Babcock, author of *Women Don't Ask*.

The term "gig economy" refers to the growing number of Americans who are working on a per-project or freelance basis. Often in the gig economy, a person has mini-jobs. The worker might work a few hours on one project and perform an entirely different task for another project.

Some people work in the gig economy by choice. Working on multiple projects can keep work interesting and help develop a variety of useful skills. The gig economy is flexible, giving workers more freedom to work when and where they want. But there are also many workers in the gig economy who would like a full-time permanent job but can't find one.

More people joined the gig economy during the Great Recession of 2007–2009, when employers reduced costs by laying off workers or hiring temporary help. New businesses such as TaskRabbit popped up. TaskRabbit.com matches people who need help with odd jobs with people who are looking to earn a little cash.

In better economic times, fewer workers tend to work on a per-project basis as companies start hiring permanent employees again. However, advances in technology that make it easier for workers to work remotely, and a growing number of people who want a better work-life balance, point to the gig economy's permanent place in the work world.

Most of us have many ideas about what we want to be as we grow older and our interests change. Picking a career that we like and that will allow us to earn a good income is the key to success. Do well in high school and earn a college degree in a major with good job prospects, and you're likely to find more career opportunities.

If you are itching to be your own boss, there are many resources out there to help you, from Junior Achievement to the volunteer mentors of the Small Business Administration's SCORE Association. Just think, all major corporations once started with the kernel of an idea.

An idea, an entrepreneurial spirit, perseverance, and hard work can take you far. And always remember that millionaires who spend more than they make are worse off than average people who live within their means. Saving money and making savvy decisions about the money you spend are just as important as earning it.

GLOSSARY

bachelor's degree—a degree from a college or university, usually completed in four years

capital—amount of money needed to start a business or complete a project

commission—payment based on a percentage of sales

entrepreneur—person who starts a business or company

freelance—to work for multiple companies, usually with a contract that lasts a certain amount of time or on a per-project basis

gross pay—total amount of money earned before taxes and benefit costs are deducted

intern—person who works for little or no money to gain experience

median—middle; half of workers make more than the median income and half of workers make less

negotiate—to bargain or discuss something in order to come to an agreement

network—to contact other people in the same industry in order to find a job

recession—temporary slowing of business activity

résumé—document that lists an employee's education, work experience, and skills

salary—fixed amount of earnings per pay period

FURTHER READING

Chatzky, Jean Sherman. *Not Your Parents' Money Book: Making, Saving, and Spending Your Own Money.* New York: Simon & Schuster Books for Young Readers, 2010.

Karchut, Wes, and Darby Karchut. *Money and Teens: Savvy Money Skills.* Colorado Springs, Colo.: Copper Square Studios, 2012.

Sethi, Ramit. *I Will Teach You to be Rich.* New York: Workman Pub., 2009.

INTERNET SITES

Use FactHound to find Internet sites related to this book. All of the sites on FactHound have been researched by our staff.

Here's all you do:

Visit *www.facthound.com*

Type in this code:
9780756543723

OTHER SITES TO EXPLORE

Junior Achievement
https://www.juniorachievement.org/web/ja-usa/home

The Mint
http://www.themint.org

Teen Business Link
http://archive.sba.gov/teens/

U.S. Department of Labor
http://www.dol.gov

Bestprep. 1 May 2014.
http://bestprep.org

Brookings. Quality. Independence.
Impact. 1 May 2014.
http://www.brookings.edu

Casey Lewis. "What to Wear to a
Job Interview." *Teen Vogue*. 9 May
2014. http://www.teenvogue.com/
fashion/what-to-wear/2012-05/job-
interview/?slide=1

The College Board. 1 May 2014.
https://www.collegeboard.org

The College Payoff. Georgetown
University's Center on Education and
the Workforce. 5 Aug. 2011. 1 May
2014. http://cew.georgetown.edu/
collegepayoff

Employment Policies Institute.
1 May 2014. http://www.epionline.org

Internal Revenue Service. 1 May 2014.
http://www.irs.gov

Iseek. Minnesota's Career, Education, and
Job Resource. 1 May 2014.
http://www.iseek.org

Job Search, Interview & Employment
Advice. 1 May 2014.
http://jobsearch.about.com

Jump Start. Financial Smarts for Students.
1 May 2014. http://jumpstart.org

The Mint: Fun Financial Literacy
Activities for Kids, Teens, Parents and
Teachers. 1 May 2014.
http://www.themint.org

National Endowment for Financial
Education. 1 May 2014. www.nefe.org

Share Save Spend. Money + Meaning.
1 May 2014.
http://www.sharesavespend.com

SOURCE NOTES

Page 9, line 1: Notorious B.I.G. lyrics:
Mo Money Mo Problems. 9 May 2014.
http://www.azlyrics.com/lyrics/
notoriousbig/momoneymoproblems.
html

Page 9, line 3: Hank Williams Jr.:
"Money Can't Buy Happiness" Lyrics.
9 May 2014. http://www.sweetslyrics.
com/255474.Hank%20Williams%20
Jr.%20-%20Money%20Can't%20Buy%20
Happiness.html

Page 29, line 1: Teen Business Link. Ideas
for Your Business. U.S. Small Business
Administration. 9 May 2014. http://
archive.sba.gov/teens/ideas.html

Page 30, line 12: Teen Business Link.
Put it in Writing. U.S. Small Business
Administration. 9 May 2014. http://
archive.sba.gov/teens/myplan.html

Page 35, line 1: E-mail interview.
30 May 2013.

Page 36, line 4: Phone interview.
5 June 2013.

Page 37, line 17: "Key Skills for Youth to
Succeed and Thrive." Camp BizSmart.
9 May 2014. http://campbizsmart.
org/2013/05/16/key-skills-for-youth-to-
succeed-and-thrive/

Pages 38 and 39: Tanya Prive. "Top 32
Quotes Every Entrepreneur Should
Live By." 2 May 2013. 9 May 2014.
http://www.forbes.com/sites/
tanyaprive/2013/05/02/top-32-quotes-
every-entrepreneur-should-live-by/

Page 55, line 2: Women Don't Ask:
Negotiation and the Gender Drive. 9 May
2014. http://www.womendontask.com/
stats.html

About the Author

Kara McGuire is an award-winning personal finance writer, consumer researcher, and speaker. She writes a personal finance column for the Minneapolis *Star Tribune* and formerly worked for the public radio program *Marketplace Money*. She enjoys teaching young people and parents about money. Kara lives in St. Paul, Minnesota, with her husband, Matt, and children Charlotte, Teddy, and August.